A Global Directory of Zoos and More!

Visit awesome places animals live: zoos, aquariums, nature & wildlife conservation centers, educational farms, sanctuaries, and more.

By C S Wurzberger

Want to use this Directory in your school, home schooling groups, summer camp, daycare center, library, church, girl & boy scouts, 4-h group, campground, zoo, aquarium, wildlife conservation center, or other?

Contact us at Office@AwesomeAnimalAdventures.com for bulk order quantities and discounts.

ISBN: *9798621498559*

Awesome Animal Academy, C S Wurzberger, P. O. Box 343, Marlboro, VT 05344.

AwesomeAnimalAdventures.com

This Directory is dedicated to the
Dodo Bird. May you inspire people from
around the world to meet the animals, hear
their stories, and connect with organizations
involved in protecting them from extinction!

US Regions

TABLE OF CONTENT

INTRODUCTION

Something amazing happens to people in the presence of animals. They are calmer, more curious, and more joyful.

Animals support a person's emotional health by giving unconditional love, comfort and security, and teaching them about empathy, compassion, confidence, and responsibility.

Here are 3 ways to brighten your day while connecting with the animals you love and the ones you are yet to meet:

1. Use this printed Global Directory when planning your vacation. This U.S. Edition is divided up by regions, states, and cities.

   PS. Other editions for Canada, South America, Europe, Australia, and others will be available late 2020.

2. Explore the Global Online Directory at: AwesomeAnimalAdventures.com

In the online version, you'll find it to be the most comprehensive directory available on the Internet. You can search for places, view pictures & videos of the animals, visit the location's website, get directions, and connect with them through their social media links.

3. Travel virtually at <u>AwesomeAnimalAdventures.tv</u> from the comfort of your couch, classroom or back seat. You'll go behind the scenes with your guide C S Wurzberger to meet the animals, hear their stories, and connect with people and organizations working to care for them.

Enjoy your Awesome Animal Adventures!

NORTHEAST

Connecticut, Delaware, Maine, Massachusetts, Maryland, New Hampshire, New Jersey, New York, Pennsylvania, Rhode Island, and Vermont.

- - Connecticut

BRIDGEPORT

Connecticut's Beardsley Zoo
1875 Noble Avenue
Bridgeport, CT 06610-1600
Website: http://www.beardsleyzoo.org/

CANTON

Roaring Brook Nature Center
70 Gracey Road
Canton, CT 06019
Website: http://www.roaringbrook.org/

DARIEN

The Darien Nature Center
120 Brookside Road
Darien, CT 06820
Website: https://dariennaturecenter.org/

MYSTIC

Mystic Aquarium & Institute for Exploration
55 Coogan Blvd
Mystic, CT 06355-1997
Website: http://www.mysticaquarium.org/

NORWALK

Maritime Aquarium
10 North Water Street
Norwalk, CT 06854
Website: https://www.maritimeaquarium.org/

SHARON

Audubon-Sharon Audubon Center
325 Cornwall Bridge Road
Sharon, CT 06069
Website: https://sharon.audubon.org/

- - Delaware

TOWNSEND

3 Palms Zoo & Education Center
1060 Vandyke Greenspring Road
Townsend, DE 19734
Website: https://3palmszoo.org/

WILMINGTON

Brandywine Zoo
1001 N. Park Drive
Wilmington, DE 19802-3801
Website: http://www.brandywinezoo.org/

- - Maine

GRAY

Maine Wildlife Park
56 Game Farm Road
Gray, ME 04039
Website: https://www.maine.gov/ifw/wildlife-park/index.html

MOUNT VERNON

York's Wild Kingdom
918 Pond Road
Mount Vernon, ME 04352
Website: http://dewhaven.com/

BOOTHBAY HARBOR

Maine State Aquarium
McKown Point Road
Boothbay Harbor, ME 04538
Website: https://www.maine.gov/dmr/education/aquarium/index.html

YORK BEACH

York's Wild Kingdom
1 Animal Park Road
York Beach, ME 03909
Website: http://www.yorkzoo.com/

- - Massachusetts

ATTLEBORO

Capron Park Zoo
201 County Street
Attleboro, MA 02703-3510
Website: http://www.capronparkzoo.com/

BOSTON

Franklin Park Zoo
1 Franklin Park Road
Boston, MA 02121-3255
Website: http://www.zoonewengland.org/franklin-park-zoo

Museum of Science
Science Park
Boston, MA 02114-1099
Website: http://www.mos.org/

New England Aquarium
Central Wharf
Boston, MA 02110-3399
Website: http://www.neaq.org/

LUDLOW

Lupa Zoo
62 Nash Hill Road
Ludlow, MA 01056
Website: https://www.lupazoo.org/

MENDON

Southwick's Zoo
2 Southwick Street
Mendon, MA 01756
Website: http://southwickszoo.com/

NANTUCKET

Maria Mitchell Aquarium
28 Washington Street
Nantucket, MA 02554
Website: http://www.mariamitchell.org/visit/aquarium

NEW BEDFORD

Buttonwood Park Zoo
425 Hawthorn Street
New Bedford, MA 02740
Website: http://bpzoo.org/

SPRINGFIELD

Zoo in Forest Park
293 Sumner Avenue
Springfield, MA 01108
Website: https://www.forestparkzoo.org/

STONEHAM

Stone Zoo
149 Pond Street
Stoneham, MA 02180
Website: http://www.zoonewengland.org/stone-zoo

WOODS HOLE

Woods Hole Science Aquarium
166 Water Street
Woods Hole, MA 02543
Website: https://www.fisheries.noaa.gov/new-england-mid-atlantic/outreach-and-education/woods-hole-science-aquarium

- - Maryland

BALTIMORE

National Aquarium in Baltimore
501 E. Pratt Street, Pier 3
Baltimore, MD 21202-3194
Website: https://aqua.org/

The Maryland Zoo in Baltimore
Druid Hill Park
Baltimore, MD 21217
Website: http://www.marylandzoo.org/

RISING SUN

Plumpton Park Zoo
1416 Telegraph Road
Rising Sun, MD 21911
Website: https://plumptonparkzoo.org/

SALISBURY

Salisbury Zoological Park
755 South Park Drive
Salisbury, MD 21802-2979
Website: http://www.salisburyzoo.org/

THURMONT

Catoctin Wildlife Preserve
13019 Catoctin Furnace Road
Thurmont, MD 21788
Website: https://catoctinwildlifepreserve.com/

--New Hampshire

CANDIA

Charmingfare Farm
774 High Street
Candia, NH 03034
Website: https://www.visitthefarm.com/

HOLDERNESS

Squam Lake Natural Science Center
23 Science Center Road
Holderness, NH 03245-0173
Website: https://www.nhnature.org/

- - New Jersey

BRIDGETON

Cohanzick Zoo
45 Mayor Aitken Drive
Bridgeton, NJ 08302
Website: http://cohanzickzoo.org/

CAMDEN

Adventure Aquarium
1 Aquarium Drive
Camden, NJ 08103-1060
Website: http://www.adventureaquarium.com/

CAPE MAY COURT HOUSE

Cape May County Park Zoo
Route 9 & Pine Lane
Cape May Court House, NJ 08210
Website: https://www.capemaycountynj.gov/1008/Park-Zoo

FORKED RIVER

Popcorn Park Zoo
1 Humane Way
Forked River, NJ 08731
Website: https://www.ahscares.org

PARAMUS

Bergen County Zoological Park
216 Forest Avenue
Paramus, NJ 07652-5349
Website: https://www.co.bergen.nj.us/bergen-county-zoo/about-bergen-county-zoo

POINT PLEASANT BEACH

Jenkinson's Aquarium
300 Ocean Avenue
Point Pleasant Beach, NJ 08742-3621
Website: http://jenkinsons.com/aquarium/

SUSSEX

Space Farms: Zoo & Museum
218 County Road
Sussex, NJ 07461

Website: https://www.spacefarms.com/

WEST ORANGE

Turtle Back Zoo
560 Northfield Avenue
West Orange, NJ 07052
Website: http://turtlebackzoo.com/

- - New York

BINGHAMTON

Ross Park Zoo
60 Morgan Road
Binghamton, NY 13903
Website: https://rossparkzoo.org/

BRONX

Bronx Zoo
2300 Southern Blvd
Bronx, NY 10460-1090
Website: http://bronxzoo.com/

BROOKLYN

New York Aquarium
Surf Avenue at West 8th Street
Brooklyn, NY 11224-2899
Website: http://nyaquarium.com/

Prospect Park Zoo

450 Flatbush Avenue

Brooklyn, NY 11225-3707

Website: http://prospectparkzoo.com/

BUFFALO

Buffalo Zoo

300 Parkside Avenue

Buffalo, NY 14214-1999

Website: http://www.buffalozoo.org/

COLD SPRING HARBOR

Cold Spring Harbor Fish Hatchery & Aquarium

1660 Rte 25A

Cold Spring Harbor, NY 11724

Website: http://cshfishhatchery.org/

FLUSHING

Queens Zoo

5351 111th Street

Flushing, NY 11368-3301

Website: http://queenszoo.com/

GLOVERSVILLE

Adirondack Animal Land
3554 State HWY R30
Gloversville, NY 12025
Website: http://www.adirondackanimalland.com/

HARPURSVILLE

Animal Adventure Park
85 Martin Hill Road
Harpursville, NY 13787
Website: https://theanimaladventurepark.com/

MILLBROOK

Trevor Zoo
131 Millbrook School Road
Millbrook, NY 12545-9797
Website: https://www.millbrook.org/trevor-zoo-home

NEW YORK

Central Park Zoo
830 5th Avenue
New York, NY 10065-7001
Website: http://centralparkzoo.com/

NIAGARA

Aquarium of Niagara
701 Whirlpool Street
Niagara Falls, NY 14301
Website: https://www.aquariumofniagara.org/

ONEONTA

Joseph L. Popp Jr. Butterfly Conservatory
5802 State Highway 7
Oneonta, NY 13820
Website: N/A

ROCHESTER

Seneca Park Zoo
2222 St. Paul Street
Rochester, NY 14621-1097
Website: http://senecaparkzoo.org/

ROME

Fort Rickey Children's Discovery Zoo
5135 Rome-New London Road
Rome, NY 14621-1097
Website: https://fortrickey.com/

SAUGERTIES

Catskill Animal Sanctuary
316 Old Stage Road
Saugerties, NY 12477
Website: https://casanctuary.org/

SCARSDALE

Greenburgh Nature Center
99 Dromore Rd
Scarsdale, NY 10583
Website: http://www.greenburghnaturecenter.org/

SCHENECTADY

Via Aquarium
93 W. Campbell Road
Schenectady, NY 12306
Website: https://viaaquarium.com/

STATEN ISLAND

Staten Island Zoo
614 Broadway
Staten Island, NY 10310-2896
Website: http://statenislandzoo.org/

SYRACUSE

Rosamond Gifford Zoo at Burnet Park
One Conservation Place
Syracuse, NY 13204-2590
Website: http://www.rosamondgiffordzoo.org/

TUPPER LAKE

Wild Center and Wild Walk
45 Museum Drive
Tupper Lake, NY 12986
Website: https://www.wildcenter.org/

UTICA ZOO

Utica Zoo
1 Utica Zoo Way
Utica, NY 13501
Website: http://uticazoo.org/

VARYSBURG

Hidden Valley Animal Adventure
2887 Royce Road
Varysburg, NY 14167
Website: https://hiddenvalleyadventure.com/

WATERTOWN

New York State Zoo at Thompson Park
1 Thompson Park
Watertown, NY 13601
Website: https://www.nyszoo.org/

WILMINGTON

Adirondack Wildlife Refuge
977 Springfield Road
Wilmington, NY 12997
Website: http://www.adirondackwildlife.org/

- - Pennsylvania

ALLENWOOD

Clyde Peeling's Reptiland
18628 US Route 15
Allenwood, PA 17810
Website: http://reptiland.com/

ERIE

Erie Zoo
423 West 38th Street
Erie, PA 16508
Website: http://www.eriezoo.org

HALIFAX

Lake Tobias Wildlife Park
760 Tobias Drive
Halifax, PA 17032
Website: https://www.laketobias.com/

HERSHEY

Zoo America North America Wildlife Park
Park Blvd & Route 743 N.
Hershey, PA 17033
Website: http://www.zooamerica.com/

LAKE ARIEL

Claws N' Paws Wild Animal Park
1475 Ledgedale Road
Lake Ariel, PA 18436
Website: http://www.clawsnpaws.com/

LITITZ

Wolf Sanctuary of Pennsylvania
465 Speedwell Forge Road
Lititz, PA 17543-9537
Website: https://wolfsanctuarypa.org/

NORRISTOWN

Elmwood Park Zoo
1661 Harding Boulevard
Norristown, PA 19401-2974
Website: http://www.elmwoodparkzoo.org/

PHILADELPHIA

The Philadelphia Zoo
3400 West Girard Avenue
Philadelphia, PA 19104-1196
Website: http://www.philadelphiazoo.org/

PITTSBURGH

National Aviary
600 West Ohio Street
Pittsburgh, PA 15212
Website: https://www.aviary.org/

Pittsburgh Zoo & PPG Aquarium
One Wild Place
Pittsburgh, PA 15206-1178
Website: http://www.pittsburghzoo.org/

SCHNECKSVILLE

Lehigh Valley Zoo
5150 Game Preserve Road
Schnecksville, PA 18078-0519
Website: https://www.lvzoo.org/

- - Rhode Island

PROVIDENCE

Roger Williams Park Zoo
1000 Elmwood Avenue
Providence, RI 02907-3659
Website: http://www.rwpzoo.org/

- - Vermont

MARLBORO

Southern Vermont Natural History Museum
7599 VT Route 9
West Marlboro, VT 05363
Website: https://www.vermontmuseum.org/

QUECHEE

VINS Nature Center
149 Natures Way
Quechee, VT 05059
Website: https://vinsweb.org/

Travel Notes:

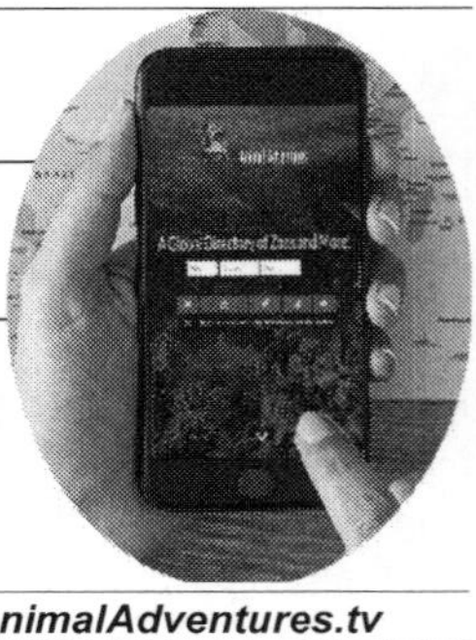

_____

_____

_____

_____

_____

_____

_____

_____

_____

_____

_____

_____

_____

_____

Visit: **AwesomeAnimalAdventures.com**

A Global Directory of Zoos and More!

SOUTHEAST

Alabama, Arkansas, Florida, Georgia, Kentucky,
Louisiana, Mississippi, North Carolina, South Carolina,
Tennessee, Virginia, and West Virginia.

--Alabama

ATTALLA

Tigers for Tomorrow at Untamed Mountain
708 County Road 345
Attalla, AL 35954
Website: https://www.tigersfortomorrow.org/

BIRMINGHAM

Birmingham Zoo
2630 Cahaba Road
Birmingham, AL 35223-1154
Website: https://www.birminghamzoo.com/

GULF SHORES

Alabama Gulf Coast Zoo
1204 Gulf Shores Parkway
Gulf Shores, AL 36542
Website: http://www.alabamagulfcoastzoo.com/

HUNTSVILLE

Harmony Park Safari
431 Clouds Cove Road SE
Huntsville, AL 35803
Website: http://www.harmonyparksafari.com/

MONTGOMERY

Montgomery Zoo
2301 Coliseum Parkway
Montgomery, AL 36109-0313
Website: http://www.montgomeryzoo.com/

SUMMERDALE

Alligator Alley
19950 Highway 71
Summerdale, AL 36580
Website: https://gatoralleyfarm.com/

- - Arkansas

EUREKA SPRINGS

Turpentine Creek Wildlife Refuge
239 Turpentine Creek Land
Eureka Springs, AR 72632
Website: https://www.turpentinecreek.org/

FORT SMITH

Arkansas River Valley Nature Center
8300 Wells Lake Road
Fort Smith, AR 72923
Website: https://www.agfc.com/en/explore-outdoors/
nature-and-education-centers/jharvnc/

GENTRY

Wild Wilderness Drive-Through Safari
20923 Safari Road
Gentry, AR 72734
Website: https://
www.wildwildernessdrivethroughsafari.com/

HOT SPRINGS

Arkansas Alligator Farm & Petting Zoo
847 Whittington Avenue
Hot Springs, AR 71901
Website: https://alligatorfarmzoo.com/

National Park Aquarium
209 Central Avenue
Hot Springs, AR 71901
Website: http://www.nationalparkaquarium.org/

LITTLE ROCK

Little Rock Zoo
1 Zoo Drive
Little Rock, AR 72205-5401
Website: http://littlerockzoo.com/

MANILA

Big Lake National Wildlife Refuge
2274 Highway 18
Manila, AR 72442
Website: https://www.fws.gov/refuge/big_lake/

- - Florida

GAINESVILLE

Santa Fe College Teaching Zoo
3000 NW 83rd Street
Gainesville, FL 32606-6200
Website: http://www.sfcollege.edu/zoo/

JACKSONVILLE

Jacksonville Zoo and Gardens
370 Zoo Parkway
Jacksonville, FL 32218-5799
Website: http://www.jacksonvillezoo.org/

LOXAHATCHEE

Lion Country Safari
2003 Lion Country Safari Road
Loxahatchee, FL 33470-3977
Website: http://www.lioncountrysafari.com/

MELBOURNE

Brevard Zoo
8225 N. Wickham Road
Melbourne, FL 32940-7924
Website: https://brevardzoo.org/

NAPLES

Naples Zoo
1590 Goodlette-Frank Road
Naples, FL 43102-5260
Website: http://www.napleszoo.org/

ORLANDO

Sea World Orlando
7007 Sea World Drive
Orlando, FL 32821-8097
Website: https://seaworld.org/

SARASOTA

Mote Marine Aquarium
1600 Ken Thompson Parkway
Sarasota, FL 34236-1096
Website: https://mote.org/

SILVER SPRINGS

Forest Animal Rescue
640 NE 170th Court
Silver Springs, FL 34488
Website: https://www.forestanimalrescue.org/

ST. AUGUSTINE

St. Augustine Alligator Farm
999 Anastasia Blvd
St. Augustine, FL 32080
Website: http://www.alligatorfarm.com/

TAMPA

Florida Aquarium
701 Channelside Drive
Tampa, FL 33602-5614
Website: http://www.flaquarium.org/

Tampa's Lowry Park Zoo
1101 W. Sligh Avenue
Tampa, FL 33604-5958
Website: http://www.lowryparkzoo.org/

WEST PALM BEACH

Palm Beach Zoo
1301 Summit Blvd
West Palm Beach, FL 33405-3035
Website: http://www.palmbeachzoo.org/

- - Georgia

ALBANY

Chehaw Wild Animal Park
105 Chehaw Park Road
Albany, GA 31701-1260
Website: http://chehaw.org/

ATLANTA

Georgia Aquarium
225 Baker Street
Atlanta, GA 30313
Website: http://www.georgiaaquarium.org/

Zoo Atlanta
800 Cherokee Avenue SE
Atlanta, GA 30315-1440
Website: http://www.zooatlanta.org/

CLEVELAND

North Georgia Zoo & Farm
2912 Paradise Valley Road
Cleveland, GA 30528
Website: https://www.northgeorgiazoo.com/

DAHLONEGA

Chestatee Wildlife Preserve & Zoo
469 Old Dahlonega Highway
Dahlonega, GA 30533
Website: https://chestateewildlife.com/

LOCUST GROVE

Noah's Ark Animal Sanctuary
712 L G Griffin Road
Locust Grove, GA 30248
Website: http://www.noahs-ark.org/

PINE MOUNTAIN

Wild Animal Safari, Inc
1300 Oak Grove Road
Pine Mountain, GA 31822
Website: https://animalsafari.com/Georgia/

SAVANNAH

Savannah Zoo
711 Sandtown Road
Savannah, GA 31410
Website: http://www.savannahzoo.org/

- - Kentucky

HORSE CAVE

Kentucky Down Under Adventure Zoo
3700 L & N Turnpike Road
Horse Cave, KY 42749
Website: https://www.kentuckydownunder.com/

LEXINGTON

Kentucky Wildlife Center
4270 Georgetown Road
Lexington, KY 40511
Website: https://www.kywildlife.org/

LOUISVILLE

Louisville Zoological Garden
1100 Trevillian Way
Louisville, KY 40213-1559
Website: https://louisvillezoo.org/

NEWPORT NEWS

Newport Aquarium
One Aquarium Way
Newport News, KY 41071-1679
Website: http://www.newportaquarium.com/

SLADE

Kentucky Reptile Zoo
200 L & E Railroad Place
Slade, KY 40376
Website: http://www.kyreptilezoo.org

- - Louisiana

ALEXANDRIA

Alexandria Zoological Park
3016 Masonic Drive
Alexandria, LA 71301-4240
Website: http://www.thealexandriazoo.com/

BATON ROUGE

BREC's Baton Rouge Zoo
3601 Thomas Road
Baton Rouge, LA 70807
Website: http://www.brzoo.org/

BROUSSARD

Zoosiana
5601 Hwy 90 E.
Broussard, LA 70518
Website: https://zoosiana.com/

DELHI

Wild Country Safari Park
8 Hobby Newton Road
Delhi, LA 71232
Website: https://www.wildcountrysafari.com/

NEW ORLEANS

Audubon Aquarium of the Americas
1 Canal Street
New Orleans, LA 70130-1175
Website: http://audubonnatureinstitute.org/aquarium/

Audubon Zoo
6500 Magazine Street
New Orleans, LA 70178-4327
Website: http://audubonnatureinstitute.org/

PINEVILLE

Gone Wild Safari
805 Hooper Road
Pineville, LA 71360
Website: http://gonewildsafari.com/

SHREVEPORT

Shreveport Aquarium
601 Clyde Fant Pkwy
Shreveport, LA 71101
Website: https://www.shreveportaquarium.com/

- - Mississippi

GULFPORT

Mississippi Aquarium
2100 E Beach Blvd
Gulfport, MS 39501
Website: https://www.msaquarium.org/

HATTIESBURG

Hattiesburg Zoo
107 S 17th Avenue
Hattiesburg, MS 39401
Website: https://hattiesburgzoo.com/

JACKSON

Jackson Zoological Park
2918 W. Capital Street
Jackson, MS 39209-4293
Website: http://jacksonzoo.org/

TUPELO

Tupelo Buffalo Park & Zoo
2272 N Coley Road
Tupelo, MS 38801
Website: http://www.tupelobuffalopark.com/

- - North Carolina

ASHEBORO

North Carolina Zoological Park
4401 Zoo Parkway
Asheboro, NC 27205-1425
Website: https://www.nczoo.org/

ASHEVILLE

Website: http://www.nczoo.org/
Western North Carolina Nature Center
75 Gashes Creek Road
Asheville, NC 28805-2529
Website: http://www.wncnaturecenter.com/

CONCORD

Sea Life Centre Charlotte
8111 Concord Mills Blvd
Concord, NC 28027
Website: https://www.visitsealife.com/charlotte-concord/

GREENSBORO

Natural Science Center & Animal Discovery of Greensboro
4301 Lawndale Drive
Greensboro, NC 27455
Website: http://www.greensboroscience.org/

KURE BEACH

North Carolina Aquarium at Fort Fisher
900 Loggerhead Road
Kure Beach, NC 28449-3786
Website: http://www.ncaquariums.com/fort-fisher

MANTEO

North Carolina Aquarium on Roanoke Island
374 Airport Road
Manteo, NC 27954
Website: http://www.ncaquariums.com/roanoke-island

PINE KNOLL SHORES

North Carolina Aquarium at Pine Knoll Shores
1 Roosevelt Drive
Pine Knoll Shores, NC 28512
Website: http://www.ncaquariums.com/pine-knoll-shores

- - South Carolina

CHARLESTON

South Carolina Aquarium
100 Aquarium Wharf
Charleston, SC 29401
Website: http://www.scaquarium.org

COLUMBIA

Riverbanks Zoo & Garden
500 Wildlife Parkway
Columbia, SC 29210
Website: http://www.riverbanks.org/

EDISTO ISLAND

Edisto Island Serpentarium
1374 SC-174
Edisto Island, SC 29438
Website: https://edistoserpentarium.com/

GREENVILLE

Greenville Zoo
150 Cleveland Park Drive
Greenville, SC 29601-3147
Website: http://www.greenvillezoo.org/

MURRELLS INLET

Brookgreen Gardens
1931 Brookgreen Drive
Murrells Inlet, SC 29576
Website: http://www.brookgreen.org/

MYRTLE BEACH

Ripley's Aquarium
1110 Celebrity Circle
Myrtle Beach, SC 29577-7465
Website: http://www.ripleyaquariums.com/myrtlebeach/

NORTH MYRTLE BEACH

Alligator Adventure
4604 Hwy 17 S.
North Myrtle Beach, SC 29582
Website: https://alligatoradventure.com/

WELLFORD

Hollywild Animal Park
2325 Hampton Road
Wellford, SC 29385577-7465
Website: https://www.hollywild.org/

- - Tennessee

CHATTANOOGA

Chattanooga Zoo at Warner Park
301 N Holtzclaw Ave.
Chattanooga, TN 37404-2303
Website: http://www.chattzoo.org/

Tennessee Aquarium
One Broad Street
Chanttanooga, TN 37401
Website: http://www.tennesseeaquarium.org

CLINTON

Little Ponderosa Zoo & Rescue
629 Granite Road
Clinton, TN 37716
Website: https://littleponderosazoo.com/

GATLINBURG

Ripley's Aquarium of the Smokies
88 River road
Gatlinburg, TN 37738
Website: http://www.ripleyaquariums.com/gatlinburg/

KINGSTON

Tiger Haven
237 Harvey Road
Kingston, TN 37763
Website: http://www.tigerhaven.org

KNOXVILLE

Knoxville Zoological Gardens
3500 Knoxville Zoo Drive
Knoxville, TN 37914
Website: http://www.knoxville-zoo.org/

MEMPHIS

Memphis Zoo
2000 Prentiss Place
Memphis, TN 38112
Website: http://www.memphiszoo.org/

NASHVILLE

Nashville Zoo
3777 Nolensville Road
Nashville, TN 37211-3711
Website: http://www.nashvillezoo.org/

SEVIERVILLE

Smoky Mountain Deer Farm and Exotic Petting Zoo

478 Happy Hollow Lane
Sevierville, TN 37876
Website: http://deerfarmzoo.com/

- - Virginia

GATE CITY

Creation Kingdom Zoo
1692 Snowflake Road
Gate City, VA 24251
Website: http://www.creationkingdomzoo.com/

NEWPORT NEWS

Virginia Living Museum
524 J. Clyde Morris Blvd
Newport News, VA 23601
Website: http://www.thevlm.org/

NORFOLK

Virginia Zoological Park
3500 Granby Street
Norfolk, VA 23504-1329
Website: http://www.virginiazoo.org/

ROANOKE

Mill Mountain Zoo
Mill Mountain Park
Roanoke, VA 24034-3484
Website: http://www.mmzoo.org/

VIRGINIA BEACH

Virginia Aquarium & Marine Science Center
717 General Booth Blvd
Virginia Beach, VA 23451-4811
Website: http://www.virginiaaquarium.com

- - West Virginia

FRENCH CREEK

West Virginia State Wildlife Center
163 Wildlife Road
French Creek, WV 26218
Website: http://www.wvdnr.gov/wildlife/
wildlifecenter.shtm

KINGWOOD

Hovatter's Wildlife Zoo
291 Wagner Lane
Kingwood, WV 26537
Website: https://www.westvirginiazoo.com/

WHEELING

Oglebay's Good Zoo
465 Lodge Drive
Wheeling, WV 26003
Website: https://oglebay.com/good-zoo/

Travel Notes:

_____

_____

_____

_____

_____

_____

_____

_____

_____

_____

_____

_____

_____

Visit: **AwesomeAnimalAdventures.com**

A Global Directory of Zoos and More!

MIDWEST

Illinois, Indiana, Iowa, Kansas, Michigan, Minnesota, Missouri, Nebraska, North Dakota, Ohio, South Dakota, and Wisconsin.

- - Illinois

ARCOLA

Aikman Wildlife Adventure
125 N Co Road
Arcola, IL 60505
Website: https://aikmanwildlife.com/

AURORA

Phillips Park Zoo
1000 Ray Moses Drive
Aurora, IL 60505
Website: https://www.aurora-il.org/150/Phillips-Park-Zoo

BELVIDERE

Summerfield Farm and Zoo
3088 Flora Road
Belvidere, IL 61008
Website: https://summerfieldfarmandzoo.com/

BROOKFIELD

Brookfield Zoo
8400 W 31st Street
Brookfield, IL 60513
Website: https://www.czs.org/Brookfield-ZOO/Home

CHICAGO

Lincoln Park Zoo
2001 N Clark Street
Chicago, IL 60614
Website: https://www.lpzoo.org/

Shedd Aquarium
1200 S Lake Shore Drive
Chicago, IL 60605
Website: https://www.sheddaquarium.org/

COAL VALLEY

Niabi Zoo
13010 Niabi Zoo Road
Coal Valley, IL 61240
Website: https://www.niabizoo.com/

DECATUR

Scovill Zoo
71 S Country Club Road
Decatur, IL 62521
Website: https://www.decatur-parks.org/scovill-zoo/

PEORIA

Peoria Zoo
2320 N Prospect Road
Peoria, IL 61603
Website: https://www.peoriazoo.org/

WHEATON

Cosley Zoo
1356 N Gary Avenue
Wheaton, IL 60187
Website: https://cosleyzoo.org/

--Indiana

BATTLE GROUND

Wolf Park
4004 E 800 N
Battleground, IN 47920
Website: http://wolfpark.org/

EVANSVILLE

Mesker Park Zoo & Botanic Garden
1545 Mesker Park Drive
Evansville, IN 47720-8206
Website: http://www.meskerparkzoo.com/

FORT WAYNE

Fort Wayne Children's Zoo
3411 Sherman Blvd
Fort Wayne, IN 46808-1594
Website: http://www.kidszoo.org/

INDIANAPOLIS

Indianapolis Zoo
1200 West Washington Street
Indianapolis, IN 46222
Website: https://www.indianapoliszoo.com

LAFAYETTE

Columbian Park Zoo
1915 Scott Screet
Lafayette, IN 47904
Website: http://columbianparkzoo.org/

MICHIGAN CITY

Washington Park Zoo
115 Lakeshore Drive
Michigan City, IN 46360
Website: http://washingtonparkzoo.com/

- - Iowa

DES MOINES

Blank Park Zoo
7401 SW 9th Street
Des Moines, IA 50315
Website: https://www.blankparkzoo.com/

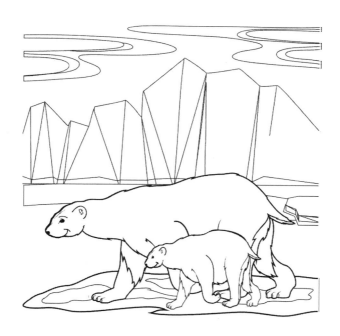

--Kansas

EMPORIA

David Traylor Zoo
75 Soden Road
Emporia, KS 66801
Website: http://www.emporiazoo.org/

GARDEN CITY

Lee Richardson Zoo
312 E Finnup Drive
Garden City, KS 67847
Website: https://www.leerichardsonzoo.org/

GODDARD

Tanganyika Wildlife Park
1000 S. Hawkins Lane
Goddard, KS 67052
Website: https://www.twpark.com/

HUTCHINSON

Hutchinson Zoo
6 Emerson Loop
Hutchinson, KS 67501
Website: http://www.hutchinsonzoo.org/

MANHATTAN

Sunset Zoo
2333 Oak Street
Manhattan, KS 66502
Website: http://www.sunsetzoo.com/

SALINA

Rolling Hills Zoo
625 N Hedville Road
Salina, KS 67401
Website: https://www.rollinghillszoo.org/

TOPEKA

Topeka Zoo
635 SW Gage Blvd.
Topeka, KS 66606
Website: https://topekazoo.org/

WICHITA

Sedgwick County Zoo
5555 W Zoo Blvd
Wichita, KS 67212
Website: https://scz.org/

- - Michigan

BATTLE CREEK

Binder Park Zoo
7400 Division Drive
Battle Creek, MI 49014-9500
Website: http://www.binderparkzoo.org/

GRAND RAPIDS

John Ball Zoological Garden
1300 W. Fulton Street
Grand Rapids, MI 49504-6100
Website: http://www.johnballzoosociety.org/

LANSING

Potter Park Zoo
1301 S Pennsylvania Avenue
Lansing, MI 48912
Website: https://potterparkzoo.org/

ROYAL OAK

Detroit Zoological Park
8450 West 10 Mile Road
Royal Oak, MI 48067-3001
Website: http://www.detroitzoo.org/

WILLIAMSBURG

GT Butterfly House & Bug Zoo
8840 M-72
Willamsburg, MI 49690
Website: http://www.gtbutterflyzoo.com/

- - Minnesota

APPLE VALLEY

Minnesota Zoological Garden
13000 Zoo Boulevard
Apple Valley, MN 55124
Website: http://www.mnzoo.org/

BRAINERD

Safari North Wildlife Park
8493 State Highway 371
Brainerd, MN 56401
Website: https://www.safarinorth.com/

DULUTH

Lake Superior Zoo
7210 Fremont Street
Duluth, MN 55807
Website: https://lszooduluth.org/

FREEPORT

Hemker Park & Zoo
26715 Co Rd 39
Freeport, MN 56331
Website: https://hemkerzoo.com/

LITTLE FALLS

Pine Grove Zoo
1200 Broadway W.
Little Falls, MN 56345
Website: https://www.pinegrovezoo.com/

MEDFORD

Reptile & Amphibian Discovery Zoo
6750 W Frontage Road
Medford, MN 55049
Website: http://www.theradzoo.com/

ROSEVILLE

SeaQuest Roseville
1595 Highway 36 West, Suite 578
Roseville, MN 55113
Website: https://roseville.visitseaquest.com/

ST PAUL

Como Park Zoo & Conservatory
1225 Estabrook Drive
St Paul, MN 55103
Website: https://comozooconservatory.org/

- - Missouri

EUREKA

Endangered Wolf Center
6750 Tyson Valley Road
Eureka, MO 63025
Website: https://www.endangeredwolfcenter.org/

KANSAS CITY

Kansas City Zoo
6800 Zoo Drive
Kansas City, MO 64123
Website: http://www.kansascityzoo.org/

SPRINGFIELD

Dickerson Park Zoo
3043 North Fort
Springfield, MO 65803
Website: http://www.dickersonparkzoo.org/

Wonders of Wildlife

500 Sunshine Street
Springfield, MO 65807
Website: https://wondersofwildlife.org/

STANTON

Wild Animal Adventures

2719 North Service Road East
Stanton, MO 63080
Website: http://wildanimaladventurepark.com/

ST. LOUIS

Saint Louis Zoo

One Government Drive
St. Louis, MO 63110
Website: http://www.stlzoo.org/

WRIGHT CITY

Big Joel's Safari Petting Zoo

13187 State Hwy M
Wright City, MO 63390
Website: https://www.bigjoelsafari.com/

- - Nebraska

LINCOLN

Lincoln Children's Zoo
1222 S. 27th
Lincoln, NE 68502-1800
Website: http://www.lincolnzoo.org/

OMAHA

Omaha's Henry Doorly Zoo
3701 S 10th Street
Omaha, NE 68107
Website: http://www.omahazoo.com/

- - North Dakota

BISMARCK

Dakota Zoo
602 Riverside Park Road
Bismarck, ND 58504
Website: https://www.dakotazoo.org/

FARGO

Red River Zoo
4255 23rd Ave S
Fargo, ND 58104
Website: https://redriverzoo.org/

MINOT

Roosevelt Park Zoo
1219 E Burdock Expy
Minot, ND 58701
Website: https://rpzoo.com/

- - Ohio

AKRON

Akron Zoological Park
500 Edgewood Avenue
Akron, OH 44307-2199
Website: https://www.akronzoo.org/

CINCINNATI

Cincinnati Zoo & Botanical Garden
3400 Vine Street
Cincinnati, OH 45220 – 1399
Website: http://cincinnatizoo.org/

CLEVELAND

Cleveland Metroparks Zoo
3900 Wildlife Way
Cleveland, OH 44109-3132
Website: http://www.clemetzoo.com/

CUMBERLAND

The Wilds
14000 International Road
Cumberland, OH 43732-9500
Website: http://www.thewilds.org/

DAYTON

Boonshoft Museum of Discovery
2600 DeWeese Parkway
Dayton, OH 45414-5499
Website: http://www.boonshoftmuseum.org/

PORT CLINTON

Website: http://www.akronzoo.org
African Safari Wildlife Park
267 South Lightner Road
Port Clinton, OH 43452-3851
Website: http://www.africansafariwildlifepark.com/

POWELL

Columbus Zoo And Aquarium
9990 Riverside Drive
Powell, OH 43065
Website: http://www.columbuszoo.org/

RAVENNA

Happy Trails Farm Animal Sanctuary
5623 New Milford Road
Ravenna, OH 44266
Website: https://happytrailsfarm.org/

TOLEDO

Toledo Zoological Gardens
2700 Broadway
Toledo, OH 43609
Website: http://www.toledozoo.org/

-- South Dakota

RAPID CITY

Bear Country USA
13820 US 16
Rapid City, SD 57702
Website: https://www.bearcountryusa.com/

Reptile Gardens
8955 US 16
Rapid City, SD 57702
Website: https://www.reptilegardens.com/

SIOUX FALLS

Butterfly House & Aquarium
4320 S Oxbow Avenue
Sioux Falls, SD 57106
Website: https://butterflyhouseaquarium.org//

Great Plains Zoo & Delbridge Museum of Natural History
805 S. Kiwanis Avenue
Sioux Falls, SD 57104
Website: https://greatzoo.org

WATERTOWN

Bramble Park Zoo
PO Box 910
Watertown, South Dakota
Website: http://www.brambleparkzoo.com/

- - Wisconsin

BARABOO

International Crane Foundation
PO Box 447
Baraboo, WI 53913-9445
Website: http://www.savingcranes.org/

GREEN BAY

Northeastern Wisconsin (NEW) Zoo
4418 Reforestation Road
Green Bay, WI 54313-8514
Website: http://www.newzoo.org/

MADISON

Henry Vilas Zoo
702 S. Randall Avenue
Madison, WI 53715-1600
Website: http://www.vilaszoo.org/

MILWAUKEE

Milwaukee County Zoological Gardens
10001 W. Bluemound Road
Milwaukee, WI 53226-4384
Website: http://www.milwaukeezoo.org/

RACINE

Racine Zoological Gardens
2131 North Main Street
Racine, WI 53402
Website: http://www.racinezoo.org/

Travel Notes:

_____

_____

_____

_____

_____

_____

_____

_____

_____

_____

_____

_____

_____

Visit: **AwesomeAnimalAdventures.com**

A Global Directory of Zoos and More!

SOUTHWEST

Arizona, New Mexico, Oklahoma, and Texas.

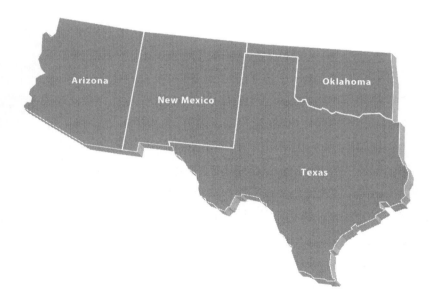

- - Arizona

CAMP VERDE

Out of Africa Wildlife Park
3505 W State Route 260
Map Verede, AZ 86322
Website: https://outofafricapark.com/

LITCHFIELD PARK

Wildlife World Zoo & Aquarium
State Route 303
Litchfield Park, AZ 85340-9466
Website: http://www.wildlifeworld.com/

PHOENIX

Phoenix Zoo
455 N. Galvin Pkwy
Phoenix, AZ 85008-3431
Website: http://www.phoenixzoo.org/

PRESCOTT

Heritage Park Zoological Sanctuary
1403 Heritage Park Road
Prescott, AZ 86301
Website: http://www.heritageparkzoo.org/

SCOTTSDALE

Southwest Wildlife Conservation Center
8711 Pinnacle Peak
Scottsdale, AZ 85255
Website: https://www.southwestwildlife.org/

TUCSON

Arizona-Sonora Desert Museum
2021 N. Kinney Road
Tucson, AZ 85743-8918
Website: http://www.desertmuseum.org/.

Reid Park Zoo
1100 S. Randolph Way
Tucson, AZ 85716
Website: http://www.tucsonzoo.org/

WILLIAMS

Bearizona

1500 E. Route 66

Williams, AZ 86046

Website: https://bearizona.com/

The Grand Canyon Deer Farm

6769 E Deer Farm Road

Williams, AZ 86046-8419

Website: https://deerfarm.com/

- - New Mexico

ALAMOGORDO

Alameda Park Zoo
1376 9th Street
Alamogordo, NM 88310
Website: https://ci.alamogordo.nm.us/477/Alameda-Park-Zoo

ALBUQUERQUE

Albuquerque Biological Park
903 10th Street
Albuquerque, NM 87102-4092
Website: http://www.cabq.gov/biopark

CARLSBAD

Living Desert Zoo & Gardens State Park
1504 Miehls Road
Carlsbad, NM 88221-0100
Website: https://www.livingdesert.org

EDGEWOOD

Wildlife West Nature Park

87 E Frontage Road
Edgewood, NM 87015
Website: http://wildlifewest.org

- - Oklahoma

JENKS

Oklahoma Aquarium
300 Aquarium Drive
Jenks, OK 74037
Website: http://www.okaquarium.org/

OKLAHOMA CITY

Oklahoma City Zoological Park
2101 NE 50th Street
Oklahoma City, OK 73111
Website: http://www.okczoo.com/

TULSA

Tulsa Zoo and Living Museum
5701 E. 36th Street N
Tulsa, OK 74115
Website: http://www.tulsazoo.com/

- - Texas

ABILENE

Abilene Zoological Gardens
2070 Zoo Lane
Abilene, TX 79602-1996
Website: http://www.abilenezoo.org/

AUSTIN

Austin Zoo
10808 Rawhide Trail
Austin, TX 78736
Website: https://austinzoo.org/

BROWNSVILLE

Gladys Porter Zoo
500 Ringgold Street
Brownsville, TX 78520-7998
Website: http://www.gpz.org/

CORPUS CHRISTI

Texas State Aquarium
2710 N. Shoreline Boulevard
Corpus Christi, TX 78402-1097
Website: http://www.texasstateaquarium.org/

DALLAS

Dallas Zoo
650 S. R.L. Thornton Freeway
Dallas, TX 75203-3013
Website: http://www.dallaszoo.com/

Dallas World Aquarium
1801 N.Griffin Street
Dallas, TX 75202
Website: http://www.dwazoo.com/

ELGIN

Dreamtime Animal Sanctuary
556 Roemer Road
Elgin, TX 78621
Website: https://www.dreamtimesanctuary.org/

EL PASO

El Paso Zoo
4001 E. Paisano Drive
El Paso, TX 79905-4223
Website: http://www.elpasozoo.org/

FORT WORTH

Fort Worth Zoo
1989 Colonial Parkway
Fort Worth, TX 6110-6640
Website: https://www.fortworthzoo.org

GLEN ROSE

Fossil Rim Wildlife Center
2155 County Road 2008
Glen Rose, TX 76043
Website: http://www.fossilrim.org/

GALVESTON

Aquarium & Rainforest at Moody Gardens, Inc.
1 Hope Boulevard
Galveston, TX 77554-8928
Website: http://www.moodygardens.com/

HOUSTON

Houston Aquarium, Inc.
410 Bagby Street
Houston, TX 77002
Website: http://www.aquariumrestaurants.com/
downtownaquariumhouston/default.asp

Houston Zoo, Inc.
1513 Cambridge Street
Houston, TX 77030-1603
Website: http://www.houstonzoo.org/

LUFKIN

Ellen Trout Zoo
402 Zoo Circle
Lufkin, TX 75904-1345
Website: http://cityoflufkin.com/zoo/

SAN ANTONIO

San Antonio Zoological Gardens & Aquarium
3903 N. Saint Mary's Street
San Antonio, TX 78212-3199
Website: https://sazoo.org

SeaWorld San Antonio
10500 SeaWorld Drive
San Antonio, TX 78251-3002
Website: http://www.seaworld.org/

TYLER

Caldwell Zoo
2203 Martin Luther Kind Blvd.
Tyler, TX 75702
Website: https://caldwellzoo.org

WACO

Cameron Park Zoo
1701 N. 4th Street
Waco, TX 76707-2463
Website: http://www.cameronparkzoo.com

WYLIE

InSync Exotics
3430 Skyview Dirve
Wylie, TX 75098
Website: https://www.insyncexotics.org/

Travel Notes:

Visit: **AwesomeAnimalAdventures.com**
A Global Directory of Zoos and More!

WEST

Alaska, California, Colorado, Hawaii, Idaho, Montana, Nevada, Oregon, Utah, Washington, and Wyoming.

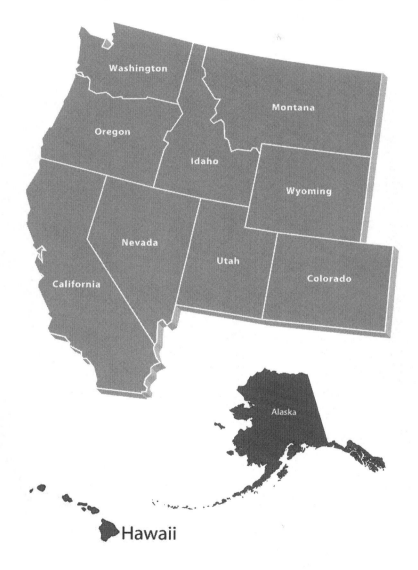

- - Alaska

ANCHORAGE

Alaska Zoo
4731 O'Malley Road
Anchorage, AK 99507
Website: https://www.alaskazoo.org/

GIRDWOOD

Alaska Wildlife Conservation Center
79 Seward Hwy
Girdwood, AK 99587
Website: https://www.alaskawildlife.org/

SEWARD

Alaska SeaLife Center
301 Railway Avenue
Seward, AK 99664
Website: https://www.alaskasealife.org/

- - California

ACTON

Shambala
6867 Soledad Canyon Road
Acton, CA 93510
Website: http://shambala.org

ALPINE

Lions Tigers & Bears
24402 Martin Way
Alpine, CA 91901
Website: https://www.lionstigersandbears.org/

ATASCADERO

Charles Paddock Zoo
9305 Pismo Avenue
Atascadero, CA 93442-4939
Website: http://www.charlespaddockzoo.org/

ESCONDIDO

San Diego Zoo Safari Park
15500 San Pasqual Valley Road
Escondido, CA 92027-7017
Website: https://www.sdzsafaripark.org

EUREKA

Sequoia Park Zoo
531 K. Street
Eureka, CA 95501-1146
Website: http://www.sequoiaparkzoo.net/

FRESNO

Fresno Chaffee Zoo
894 W. Belmont Avenue
Fresno, CA 93728-2891
Website: http://www.fresnochaffeezoo.org/

LA JOLLA

Birch Aquarium at Scripps Institute of Oceanography
9500 Gilman Drive, Dept. 0207
La Jolla, CA 92093-0207
Website: https://aquarium.ucsd.edu

LONG BEACH

Aquarium of the Pacific
100 Aquarium Way
Long Beach, CA 90802-8126
Website: http://www.aquariumofpacific.org/

LOS ANGELES

Los Angeles Zoo and Botanical Gardens
5333 Zoo Drive
Los Angeles, CA 90027-1498
Website: http://www.lazoo.org/

MONTEREY

Monterey Bay Aquarium
886 Cannery Row
Monterey, CA 93940-1085
Website: http://www.montereybayaquarium.org/

OAKLAND

Oakland Zoo
9777 Golf Links Road
Oakland, CA 94605-0238
Website: http://www.oaklandzoo.org/

PALM DESERT

Living Desert
47900 Portola Avenue
Palm Desert, CA 92260-5694
Website: http://www.livingdesert.org/

SACRAMENTO

Sacramento Zoo
3930 W. Land Park Drive
Sacramento, CA 95822-1123
Website: https://www.saczoo.org

SAN DIEGO

San Diego Zoo
2920 Zoo Drive
San Diego, CA 92112-0551
Website: http://www.sandiegozoo.org/

Sea World San Diego
500 SeaWorld Drive
San Diego, CA 92109-7904
Website: http://www.seaworld.org/

SAN FRANCISCO

Aquarium of the Bay
The Embarcadero at Beach Street, Pier 39
San Francisco, CA 94133
Website: https://www.aquariumofthebay.org

San Francisco Zoological Gardens
1 Zoo Road
San Francisco, CA 94132-1098
Website: http://www.sfzoo.org/

Steinhart Aquarium
55 Music Concourse Drive
San Francisco, CA 94118
Website: http://www.calacademy.org/academy/exhibits/
aquarium/

SAN JOSE

Happy Hollow Zoo
1300 Senter Road
San Jose, CA 95112-2520
Website: http://www.hhpz.org/

SAN MATEO

CuriOdyssey
1651 Coyote Point Drive
San Mateo, CA 94401-1097
Website: https://curiodyssey.org

SAN PEDRO

Cabrillo Marine Aquarium
3720 Stephen M. White Drive
San Pedro, CA 90731-7012
Website: http://www.cabrillomarineaquarium.org/

SANTA ANA

Santa Ana Zoo
1801 E. Chestnut Avenue
Santa Ana, CA 92701-5001
Website: http://www.santaanazoo.org/

SANTA BARBARA

Santa Barbara Zoological Gardens
500 Ninos Drive
Santa Barbara, CA 93103-3798
Website: http://www.sbzoo.org/

- - Colorado

COLORADO SPRINGS

Cheyenne Mountain Zoo
4250 Cheyenne Mountain Zoo Road
Colorado Springs, CO 80906-5755
Website: http://www.cmzoo.org/

DENVER

Denver Zoo
2300 Steele Street
Denver, CO 80205
Website: https://www.denverzoo.org/

Landry's Downtown Aquarium-Denver
700 Water Street
Denver, CO 80211-5210
Website: http://www.aquariumrestaurants.com/
downtownaquariumdenver/default.asp

DIVIDE

Colorado Wolf and Wildlife Center
4729 Twin Rocks Road
Divide, CO 80814
Website: https://www.wolfeducation.org/

KEENESBURG

The Wild Animal Sanctuary
2999 Co Rd 53
Keenesburg, CO 80643
Website: https://www.wildanimalsanctuary.org/

PUEBLO

Pueblo Zoo
3455 Nuckolls Avenue
Pueblo, CO 81005-1234
Website: http://www.pueblozoo.org/

WESTMINSTER

Butterfly Pavilion
6252 W. 104th Avenue
Westminster, CO 80020
Website: https://butterflies.org/

- - Hawaii

HONOLULU

Honolulu Zoo
151 Kapahulu Avenue
Honolulu, HI 96815-4096
Website: http://www.honoluluzoo.org/

Waikiki Aquarium
2777 Kalakaua Avenue
Honolulu, HI 96815
Website: http://www.waikikiaquarium.org/

HILO

Panama Rainforest Zoo
800 Stainback Hwy
Hilo, HI 96720
Website: https://www.hilozoo.org/

WAILUKU

Maui Ocean Center,
192 Maalaea Road
Wailuku, HI 96793
Website: https://mauioceancenter.com/

- - Idaho

BOISE

Zoo Boise
355 Julia Davis Drive
Boise, ID 83702
Website: http://www.zooboise.org/

IDAHO FALLS

Idaho Falls Zoo at Tautphaus Park
2725 Carnival Way
Idaho Falls, ID 83402
Website: https://www.idahofallsidaho.gov/1230/Zoo

POCATELLO

Zoo Idaho
2900 South 2nd Avenue
Pocatello, ID 83204
Website: https://zooidaho.org/

- - Montana

BILLINGS

Zoo Montana
2100 S. Shiloh Road
Billings, MT 59106-3908
Website: http://www.zoomontana.org/

WEST YELLOWSTONE

Grizzly & Wolf Discovery Center
201 S. Canyon Street
West Yellowstone, MT 59758
Website: http://www.grizzlydiscoveryctr.org/

- - Nevada

HENDERSON

Lion Habitat Ranch
382 Bruner Avenue
Henderson, NV 89044
Website: https://lionhabitatranch.org/

IMLAY

Safe Haven Wildlife Sanctuary
9605 Highway 400
Imlay, NV 89418
Website: https://safehavenwildlife.com/

LAS VEGAS

Shark Reef Aquarium at Mandalay Bay
3950 Las Vegas Blvd South
Las Vegas, NV 89119-1006
Website: http://www.sharkreef.com/

Animal Ark Wildlife Sanctuary

1265 Deerlodge

Reno, NV 89508

Website: https://www.animalark.org/

- - Oregon

NEWPORT

Oregon Coast Aquarium
2820 SE Ferry Slip Road
Newport, OR 97365-5269
Website: http://aquarium.org/

PORTLAND

Oregon Zoo
4001 SW Canyon Road
Portland, OR 97221
Website: http://www.oregonzoo.org/

WINSTON

Wildlife Safari
1790 Safari Road
Winston, OR 97496
Website: http://www.wildlifesafari.net/

- - Utah

LAYTON

SeaQuest Utah
1201 N Hill Field Rd #1072
Layton, UT 84041
Website: https://utah.visitseaquest.com/

SALT LAKE CITY

Utah's Hogle Zoo
2600 Sunnyside Avenue
Salt Lake City, UT 84108-1454
Website: http://www.hoglezoo.org/

Tracy Aviary
589 East 1300 South
Salt Lake City, UT 84105-1111
Website: http://www.tracyaviary.org/

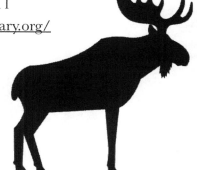

- - Washington

EATONVILLE

Northwest Trek Wildlife Park
11610 Trek Drive E.
Eatonville, WA 98328
Website: http://www.nwtrek.org/

SEATTLE

Seattle Aquarium
1483 Alaskan Way Pier 59
Seattle, WA 98101-2015
Website: http://www.seattleaquarium.org/

Woodland Park Zoo
601 N. 59th Street
Seattle, WA 98103-5858
Website: http://www.zoo.org/

TACOMA

Point Defiance Zoo & Aquarium
5400 N. Pearl Street
Tacoma, WA 98407
Website: http://www.pdza.org/

TENINO

Wolf Haven International
3111 Offut Lake Road SE
Tenino, WA 98589
Website: https://wolfhaven.org/

- - Wyoming

No locations we are aware of.

NOTE:

If you know of any animal-related places, simply send us an email with a link to their website and any contact information you can share.

We'll be glad to list them in the online directory and the next printing of the physical directory.

Contact us at: Office@AwesomeAnimalAdventures.com

Travel Notes:

Visit: **AwesomeAnimalAdventures.com**
A Global Directory of Zoos and More!

ADDITIONAL RESOURCES

Find all the animal-related information you are looking for in one simple-to-search website.

In this online Resource Hub you can click links to watch live animal cams from around the world, network with professionals in a variety of animals-related fields, and connect with organizations working to protect the animals.

Visit: AwesomeAnimalAdventures.com/resource-hub

MEET THE ANIMALS

Explore the animals you love and others you've never met?

LIVE ANIMAL CAMS

Take a peak inside and watch them living their daily lives!

NETWORKING

Come together with other professionals in the animal world!

ORGANIZATIONS

Connect with others who care about animals and conservation!

Plus, in the online Resource Hub you can discover more about the different laws that are in place to protect animals and even listen to a selection of podcasts from professionals in the field.

POLICIES & PLATFORMS

Look behind the scenes and learn more about animal welfare!

PODCASTS

Tune in and hear about conservation celebrations!

Visit:
AwesomeAnimalAdventures.com/resource-hub

MEET THE AUTHOR & HER PROGRAMS

"What we appreciate, we preserve.
What we value, we conserve.
What we are taught, we understand.
And when we understand, we can
come together to protect the
earth and its animals."
-- C S Wurzberger

C S Wurzberger

AwesomeAnimalAcademy.org
AwesomeAnimalAdventures.com
AwesomeAnimalAdventures.tv

C S Wurzberger is a Wildlife Conservation Coach,
travel blogger, author, award-winning podcaster, and
presenter with 35+ years of experience. Her passion is
connecting young people with the animals they love!

She does this through awesome animal adventures &
activities that go behind the scenes to meet the animals,
hear their stories, and connect with people and
organizations working to care for them.

Each adventure gives people a passport to the animal world. Together they explore animals, examine the facets of their livelihood, and engage in awesome animal activities that protect them and their natural habitats.

Plus, check out some of her handbooks:

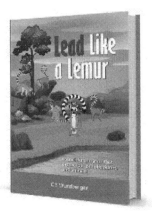

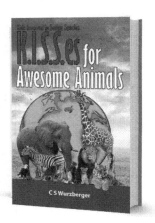

Additional handbooks and field guides can be found at
<u>AwesomeAnimalAcademy.org/handbooks</u>

C S also presents online and in person programs at selected youth organizations, Mother Earth News Fairs, zoos, aquariums, wildlife conservation centers, summer camps, and homeschooling groups throughout the world.

Bring an Awesome Animal Adventure Program to your location:

Her signature program, "K.I.S.S.es for Awesome Animals" addresses a young person's concerns about the growing number of endangered animals and the harm that is being done to their natural habitats.

Every day people are talking about how another animal is on the verge of extinction, but rarely does anyone give SPECIFIC STEPS on how to help.

This project-based program gives young people the tools they need to care for the animals they love and truly make an impact!

For more information and to book a program contact C S at office@AwesomeAnimalAcademy.org

MORE ABOUT C S:

C S is the former director of a 150-acre, 300-animal, USDA-licensed petting zoo. There she created, implemented, and promoted all their educational programs.

Plus, had the joy of bottle-raising numerous animals such as Walter the Wallaby, Parachute the Field Mouse, Ted the Cheviot Lamb, Andy the Aoudad, and many others.

After the owner retired and closed the location, C S launched out on her own to become the Founder and Director of Awesome Animal Academy.

An organization that offers in person and online leadership, stewardship, and social entrepreneurship programs for children, teens, adults, and educators who love animals and want to make a difference!

Each project-based program helps young people build confidence, grow 21st Century skills, strengthen their financial futures, and develop respect and empathy for all.

In additional Awesome Animal Academy offers hours of unplugged fun through a series of offerings (including coloring books, interactive handbooks, podcasts, project-based programs, and more!).

Give her a call at 802-258-8046 or send her an email at Office@AwesomeAnimalAcademy.org

Awesome Animal Academy
Launching Champions who Care!
AwesomeAnimalAcademy.org

Awesome Animal Adventures.tv
Your Passport to the Animal World!
AwesomeAnimalAdventures.tv

Awesome Animal Adventures
A Global Directory of Zoos and More!
AwesomeAnimalAdventures.com

Awesome Animal Advisors
Helping Zoos Showcase their In-person and Online Programs
AwesomeAnimalAdvisors.com

IS ONE OF YOUR FAVORITE PLACES MISSING FROM THIS DIRECTORY?

(zoos, aquariums, wildlife conservation centers, etc.)

Simply send us an email with a link to their website and any contact information you can share.

We'll be glad to list them in the online directory and the next printing of the physical directory.

Contact us at:

Office@AwesomeAnimalAdventures.com

Hello Fellow Awesome Animal Lovers,

I truly hope you enjoyed this directory. I sure had fun creating it for you.

I look forward to meeting you in person some day and hearing stories about your favorite animals and places.

In the meantime, feel free to reach out:
- Facebook.com/awesomeanimalacademy
- Office@AwesomeAnimalAdventures.com
- Linkedin.com/company/awesomeanimalacademy

Until then, enjoy your day and the world around you,

C S

C S Wurzberger
Wildlife Conservation Coach & Awesome Animal Advisor

Made in the USA
Columbia, SC
07 June 2020

98348979R00078